TO THE BEAT
OF THE
SPIRIT DRUM

TO THE BEAT
OF THE
SPIRIT DRUM

A Hodgepodge of Life and Spirit
Adventures

Leila Oliver White

iUniverse LLC
Bloomington

To The Beat of the Spirit Drum
A Hodgepodge of Life and Spirit Adventures

iUniverse books may be ordered through booksellers or by contacting:

iUniverse LLC
1663 Liberty Drive
Bloomington, IN 47403
www.iuniverse.com
1-800-Authors (1-800-288-4677)

ISBN: 978-1-4917-0396-0 (sc)
ISBN: 978-1-4917-0397-7 (ebk)

Printed in the United States of America

iUniverse rev. date: 08/27/2013

To my daughter Eva.
My child, my friend, my partner in crime.
I miss you, but am glad you are in a better place.

CONTENTS

Acknowledgements

Thanks to my daughter Linda McClellan without whom this book could never have happened, and to my son Harlan White who shared his adventures and Darlene Park, my granddaughter who also shared her stories with me.

Preface

When my second book came back from the publisher and was made available for sale at many book stores, I didn't think I would be able to come up with anymore subjects. I thought I had surely used every available idea and subject and that was the end of my writing.

I had much encouragement and the theories and ideas kept coming. At the end of each chapter I wondered if there would be another. It was then that memories gave me a nudge and something I thought was gone and forgotten and unimportant would creep into my mind. Then I would realize what a vast store was awaiting me. I only had to let my mind drift back to earlier times. There were many things that took place in my life that I relived and could see that it would be of interest to others.

To the Beat of the Spirit Drum

The Drum

Gift shops are so interesting, especially in Native American casinos where many of the items are hand crafted by Native Americans. While browsing in the Seven Feathers gift shop in Oregon I found many things I admired, but I kept going back to three drums of different sizes. The medium sized one kept getting my attention. After looking at the beautiful woolen blankets and robes and a fine selection of handmade jewelry I realized that I couldn't have it all. I decided on the medium sized Indian drum which hangs proudly on my wall. The other choices would have to wait until another time.

The drum is made of rawhide stretched over a frame of red cedar. It is about sixteen inches across and three inches deep. Small blocks glued together allow it to become the circular frame over which the wet rawhide is stretched. Thongs are threaded through the piece of rawhide that folds over the top of the frame and it is all pulled together underneath and becomes a braided strap. As the rawhide dries it becomes very tight.

Instructions for the care of the drum say to brush it with a light coat of Neet's foot oil every few months to help keep the top of the drum tight; damp weather can cause it to lose some of the tightness that is required. My curiosity led me to research "Neet's foot oil," and I learned that it comes from the foot of an ox. It is used to restore saddles and Western items made of leather.

My husband was lying on the bed shortly after I had purchased the drum and I was standing in the hall wiping the top of it with a paper towel after I had applied the oil when something hit it with a loud bang. Needless to say I was amazed and startled.

There were many explanations about the cause of the loud whack on the drum while I held it in my hands. Most people said it must be the change in the barometer causing the rawhide to contract or expand. Later I learned through my Spirit Guide that sound was a call to attention. The spirits wanted me to know that they were around.

Now several years later something still hits the drum occasionally with a very loud whack that raises people out of their chairs and startles them. The loudness can be compared with the sound of a small caliber rifle shot. I have learned to consult my Spirit Guide through my dowsing pendulum and alphabetical chart and see what message the spirits are bringing me. Usually they are warning me of imminent danger, to be alert.

There are still those that insist it is the changing weather causing the loud bang on the drum. I give them a knowing smile and thank the good spirits for alerting me of dangers around the area.

Introduction to the pendulum

When I first learned about pendulum dowsing I was very excited and enthusiastic. I knew about dowsing for water with a forked branch and it was as much mystery to me as it was to the scientists. I was well past middle age and retired, with time on my hands to study things and follow up the search for answers. I heard about the American Association of Dowsers headquartered in Vermont and was able to order some booklets from them with instructions for dowsing for water and lost articles. There was a local chapter of dowsers in Southern Oregon with regular meetings and my late husband and I went to one of the meetings. A friend went with us who was a science teacher interested in searching for gold. We found many uses for dowsing; you can too with these simple instructions.

MAKING A PENDULUM

The first thing to learn about pendulum dowsing is how to make a pendulum and how long the chain or string needs to be, and how to learn which are positive and negative signals.

Dowsing pendulums can be made out of many different items, from large beads with a wire loop, a steel nut from a bolt, a screw with an eye, anything that is heavy enough to swing in a circle when held at the proper length of string or chain. My favorite one is made from a clear glass or plastic bauble with a cap and a loop on top. Small pieces of stone or other bits of something can be put in the bauble, and the cap is glued around the edges. I like small bits of turquoise in it because some Native Americans say that it brings a person good luck.

I was content to be able to get positive and negative answers to my questions since I thought I had really made progress with my dowsing until my daughter Linda gave me an alphabetical dowsing chart she found in a book. The pendulum would swing to the letters and spell out sentences instead of single answers. It opened up a whole new world. I decided to put it to practical use and tried dowsing a weight loss diet. I asked the appropriate questions and got this answer: "I can help you. I am the spirit of Dr. Herman Tarnhauer, the heart surgeon who was murdered by his female assistant in New York." What a surprise that was! I followed up on the offer and was able to lose ten pounds and in doing so, I discovered that the answers to my questions were coming from the spirit world.

The pendulum became confused if I asked a question in the wrong manner or a question that could not be answered by yes or no. It went into a figure eight mode and I would have to start over again. I learned that conditions had to be favorable in order to dowse, that many things affect a person's ability to dowse, such as thunder storms, volcanic eruptions and even my state of mind! I soon learned to hold the pendulum in front me in a comfortable, relaxed position. It seemed that a better signal was received if my arm was not resting on the table.

If the string is too long, the pendulum swings slowly in a big circle. It the string is too short, it makes a small circle and spins very quickly. My own chain is about 6 inches long. For signals, it will swing clock-wise, counter clock-wise, back and forth and from side to side.

To learn your own signals, just ask the pendulum to show you the positive signal and the negative one. You only need to think the question and the pendulum will respond. After you are familiar with dowsing and have a chance to learn more about the capabilities, it is possible to learn ways to get yes and no answers without the pendulum. My eyes shift to the left if the answer is yes and shift to the right for a negative answer. I heard of one person who got answers through his fingers. He was a doctor and would hold his hand out of sight behind his desk and ask questions about his patient. A lot of doctors have used this technique; it is called radiathesia. I read about this technique in a book. You can hold your arms down at your sides and your arms will work as a pendulum. I find my signals are opposite from when I use the pendulum.

Our fingers have negative and positive polarities and are said to be reversed in left handed people. The polarities effect the action of the pendulum. As an experiment, we can hold the pendulum over one finger at a time and note the change in direction. Pendulums are very personal and should be used by only one person. They contain your magnetic energy; they should be kept in a small pouch to keep them from slipping out of your pocket and getting lost.

I asked through my dowsing chart how many people out of ten would be able to dowse successfully and the answer was six out of ten could learn to dowse and some of them could learn to communicate with the other side by learning to use the alphabet chart. The other four are inhibited either because they truly believe it will not work, or there is a conflict in their back ground that would not approve of their involvement. Another conflict is in the magnetic field that prohibits contact to be made. A location at work where a lot of electronic instruments are used will diminish a person's ability to dowse, as will a dark and gloomy atmosphere

I am not saying it was smooth sailing getting started with the dowsing chart. At first I let the pendulum follow its own course and spell out what it wanted to. It would swing back and forth and make figure eights and jerked erratically without spelling a word. It took several sessions before it calmed down enough for me to get a full sentence and what I heard was not what I expected. I was riling up some spirits of beings who expired under tragic circumstances many years ago, ghastly images I hadn't planned on meeting in this world. One was telling me a little boy was hiding in a ditch from savages that had attacked a wagon train and everyone was dead. Another session told of a drug addict that was mutilating his body because he had no feeling. Still another was a woman who had just lost her husband and she was in a state of deep grief and shock, and I was scolded furiously for interfering in her privacy. I decided that wasn't really what I wanted from the dowsing chart so I started asking specific questions that pertained only to the here and now. It smoothed out and I charged to off to a learning experience.

.A copy of the dowsing chart will be provided in the back of the book. It can be copied and laminated if desired. By laminating them they will last indefinitely, otherwise if printed on copy paper they soon become soiled and discolored. I could be more descriptive and include "rat eared" and coffee stained.

Cats, cats, cats

Whenever I start grasping for ideas for a new chapter and nothing comes to mind, there is always something about cats to fill a long space. I was not looking for cats; they just appeared on my door step and soon made it plain they wanted to stay. They looked hungry and meowed. What is a body to do? Feed them, of course.

That is not always the way it happened. One hot summer day my husband and I drove across a barren dry field and saw a beautiful yellow cat with long hair sitting by the side of the road. We remarked about it and wondered why it was just sitting there along the road. A week later we had occasion to drive by that place again and the yellow cat was still sitting in that same spot. There was no water around and nothing for it to eat except grass hoppers. There was no shade, just a dry dusty road in a stretch of barren land, several miles from the main highway.

We decided the humane thing was to take it to the main road and let it out at a house nearby. When we stopped and my husband opened the car door the cat ran up to him meowing as if to say "Please take me with you." When we got to the main road my husband decided we should take it home with us and feed it. We thought it would be a barn cat and catch mice so we fed it in the barn. The next morning it was sitting at our door. We decided it should stay close to us.

After a visit to the veterinarian and proper alterations the cat was pronounced to be in good health and he was with us for several years.

During the winter there was a deep snow storm and power outage; we watched the repair crew from the power company working in the snow a short distance from our house. I made donuts that day so we decided to walk through the snow and take some hot coffee and donuts to the crew. The yellow cat had followed us, holding his tail up high, keeping it out of the snow. He made a big hit with the crew of men and they cautioned each other to be careful and not step on the cat.

That walk through the snow that very dark night was something we remembered fondly in the years to come.

MORE ABOUT CATS

Two cats out of a litter of five survived a wild animal attack, one unscathed and one that needed some stitches. They became very special and the injured one seemed to be forever grateful and showed it with his constant desire for petting and attention. The uninjured one seemed to prefer to live at our neighbors and they welcomed him with much food until we named him "Fat Cat." Fat Cat was left with the neighbors when we moved from that area. The injured one was never really named and we just called him "Gray." He went with us wherever we moved.

One day I noticed Gray was trying to get up the steps to the porch but he first went on one side and then the other at the bottom step and I realized he was blind. I thought the reason he was always around my feet was because he wanted to be close, and then I could see that he needed my guidance.

The blindness didn't seem to be too much of a problem for him. He would go hunting around the close area and if he couldn't find his way home I would hear him meowing for help. The other two cats would fall in behind him and stay close to him. Once I watched him digging in the yard and in a short while he brought his trophy onto the porch for us to see, a nice fat shrew.

One night a cold rain came up and he got very wet and cold. I am not sure how he found his way back to his bed on the porch but the next morning I found him very wet and cold and stiff. Wondering if he was dead, I wrapped him in a warm towel and rubbed him and dried him off and soon I saw some signs of life. He lived through that ordeal and was able to survive his normal cat's life time. I have always wondered if the other cats helped him up the steps that cold wet night.

BLACK AND DECKER

My husband and I were presented with two nice kittens checked out by a veterinarian and fixed so they would not add to the cat population. One was black and one was black and white and they were playful and cute like kittens are supposed to be.

We could not think of a suitable name for them until we saw them sitting on a Black and Decker lawn mower. We named them "Black" and "Decker." I wrote a letter to the company and told them what I had done and received a tee shirt with their logo on it in the mail.

They were nice pets and we enjoyed their company. The black cat caused me to laugh so hard I could hardly get my breath I learned from him that cats can fly. It was not planned that something caused him to fly through the air; it was just a circumstance that put him into flight and caused me to laugh hysterically.

My husband had an old army Jeep from WW11 that was in the process of being restored. The muffler was worn out and the cloth top was full of holes. When my husband got into the Jeep to start it I noticed the black cat was laying on top of it sleeping peacefully in the sun. I decided I should arouse Black gently so I took a long dead stem from an iris and started to nudge him with it, but just at that very moment the Jeep motor started up with a terrible roar. The cat thought I had done something to him and he sailed through the air for about ten feet. It was several days before he would come near me again.

Whenever I feel the need to brighten the day I think of the time when I learned that cats can fly. It has given me many laughs all by myself.

LESSONS FROM THE ANIMALS

Animals really have it made. Their security system beats ours. There were six deer lounging around the edge of my yard in view from my dining room window. I couldn't help noticing that each of them was looking in a different direction, just like they were assigned a post. They must feel safe, because they lay there for hours chewing their cud and only moved their ears to detect any sounds they might hear. Sometimes some of them lay over the bank, just far enough to see a pair of ears moving once in a while.

I also notice when a hard wind blows the limbs and moss out of the oak trees, the deer eat the moss. They clean it up very quickly. Could it not be used as an emergency ration for humans when they are lost in the mountains? Apparently it has some food value. I have also noticed that deer avoid poisonous mushrooms. We should take a lesson.

Nature's fragrances

I had a demonstration of nature's fragrances recently. My son's black Lab, Cleo, often stays at my house while he is away on business. She is like a member of the family and has the run of the house. She and I were ready for our late night outing and before I let her out I checked the yard to see if there was anything that might cause trouble; a raccoon can come onto the deck and create a great commotion in the quiet of the night. Cleo went her way and I went mine across the hall, and before I let her back inside Mr. Skunk blasted off from under the house. Wow!

The blast was so strong and so fresh it made my eyes water. It seemed to come from everywhere, especially right where I sat at the computer. The odor lasted for two or three days and finally left on the breeze.

That brought to mind the little Sheltie named Fino we had for several years. I let him out early one morning. Soon a little whimpering at the door announced there had been a confrontation with a skunk. Fino was not permitted inside for a few days. It was awful. I have been told that if dogs are bathed in tomato juice it kills the odor.

The name we gave this fragrance is "Country." I wonder if the makers of fancy perfumes are envious. Some perfume ingredients are obtained from a Civet Cat, a small black animal resembling a skunk. I prefer a country breeze with a whiff of smoke in the air.

There are other country fragrances. In mid spring the wild lilacs bloom and permeate the air with a lovely odor of spring time freshness. The chaparral, also known as "Buck Brush" is a thorny bush unpopular with the farmers but in the spring it is covered with tiny white blossoms with a beautiful fragrance. The nice smell of the mountain lilies can be detected before they are seen, a nice treat for those who happen to be hiking through the mountains.

When we were children, my brothers, who were often sassy, brought our mother a bouquet of little lavender lady slippers which grew in the shady forests, true harbingers of spring. It was wonderful to see the boys' kindness showing through, which made our mother feel like the Queen that she was. The fragrance was beyond description.

MAGGIE, MY WIRE HAIRED TERRIER

I was not looking for a dog, especially a hunting dog. There she was, a cute little puppy needing a home. The people who raised her had some large hounds and the small breed of terrier was the leader of the pack.

The Wire Haired Terriers were small and fearless, relentless in the chase. Their persistence and stamina made an ideal breed for hunting wild animals. I was glad to take her away from that environment and groom her to be a nice gentle lap dog.

That was not meant to be. She tried very hard to please. I would make her into pretzel type stances and she would stay there until I told her she could move. I enjoyed taking her to the groomer who made her look like the terrier that she was, with the pointed ears that stuck up and the whiskers that are part of their charm.

She was not a one person dog. She loved the children who walked past our place and she would follow them to school or home. I always knew she was in good hands and I just waited. Usually in a couple of days I would get a phone call saying that my little dog was there and they had fed her. When we retrieved her it was obvious she had been fed, her belly stuck out like a football.

Nothing was safe around Maggie. When we finally moved back to our place in the country I tried raising some Banty chickens. She would not let them be. I would find their little lifeless bodies somewhere out in the brush where she had chased them. One time a hen had made a nest and was setting on several eggs among the bales of hay. Maggie heard them peeping when they were at the hatching stage and she found the nest and helped them along, savoring each one as she removed it from the nest. My grandchildren were visiting and came into the house with the terrible news, and bringing one surviving chic which we named "Disaster." I felt sorry for the little hen losing her little family and I cried.

My daughter next door was raising a two year old Arab filly named Twiggy. She did what horses do when dogs bite them on the heels; she retaliated by kicking. My husband and I were leaving for a short time and we left Maggie with my daughter. It was raining very hard and a big puddle had formed around an outside shed where the horse was standing. Maggie saw an opportunity to bite Twiggy on the heels and the hoof blow hit where it was aimed at Maggie's head. Maggie was knocked out cold, with her head in the puddle of water. We were just driving out the gate and my daughter wanted to try to salvage Maggie before we knew there was a problem. She carried the dog into the house where Maggie finally regained consciousness in a couple of hours, but she toppled over and wobbled around when she tried to get up.

My daughter called a veterinarian to see what should be done to save the dog. He told her nothing could be done, either the dog would live or the dog would die.

When my daughter told me she wanted to keep Maggie for a couple of days, I thought it was nice that she enjoyed the dog's company so well. I did not know my daughter was waiting for Maggie to get back to normal. Maggie did recover. A few weeks later I found a little wall plaque with a picture of a little dog with a bandage on her head which said," An act of kindness is never forgotten." It was an ideal gift for my daughter.

SNAKES GET IN THE ACT

It is hard to believe snakes were put here for a purpose when they frighten people so badly. Snakes raid bird's nests and we find that objectionable. They also help to keep down rodents. Apparently Noah saw fit to rescue them in the ark; at least they were not left behind. In the plan of things they may be getting a bad rap. I'm trying to be fair about it.

My daughter who lives next door has nice shade trees and climbing vines that make an ideal area to hang bird houses. She enjoys the flocks of little birds that roost in her trees at night. A pair of Stellar Jays comes back every year to their same nest in the vines on her deck. She watches the whole procedure from the eggs in the nest until the little ones fly away. They stay close to the area and the parent birds still feed them.

She has a nice bird house hanging near her front door, a thing of beauty with colorful designs painted on it. It is always a thrill for her to hear the baby birds first start peeping in their nest in the spring.

My daughter's sense of humor and devilish desire to play practical jokes on her family finds many outlets. Sometimes pranksters get caught in their own trap. Here is an example: A rubber snake made its rounds and several people on different occasions let out little screams and jumped back. It was a small snake but terrifying when it appeared unexpectedly, no matter where or when. One day when she stepped out on her deck she thought she was being tricked; a medium sized snake was hanging out of the bird house. She immediately thought her husband was playing a trick on her with the rubber snake. She told him "That was very good. You thought I would fall for that trick." At that point she put her hand up to pull the snake out of the bird house and it started squirming in her hand. When its tongue started darting out of its mouth she knew it was the real thing.

I was sorry to have missed the show but I imagine there were some interesting comments and exclamations that went along with the occasion.

MY ENCOUNTER WITH A REAL SNAKE

Shasta Lake in Northern California is a popular place for families to camp and swim and fish. There are many house boats and private boats, and people camp in tents along the shores of the lake.

In a normal snowy, rainy winter the lake fills to capacity and as the summers come and people use the water for irrigation the water level drops and the rocky banks get higher and higher. In a very dry season several years ago the Sacramento River could be seen at the bottom of the lake. It was a sad state of affairs for the people who had businesses around the lake.

My husband and I were not in a big boat league but were content with our small boat and motor. We enjoyed some time camping around the lake with our children when they were at home. Our dog, "Lobo" sat on the boat seat and I am sure he enjoyed the camping trips too. He was a small Collie Shepherd mix and had been with the family sine he was a small pup.

One week-end my husband and I decided to spend the night at the lake. We traveled light with the bare necessities, most of which could be carried in the picnic basket. We had a small ice chest and our sleeping bags were tightly rolled and the air mattresses flattened out so everything would fit in the small boat.

Everything had proceeded well and we were headed to a wooded spot around the lake when something went wrong with the motor. My husband could not get it started and we were marooned out in the lake far from shore. In a matter of a few minutes a nice man came along in a small boat and saw our predicament. He towed us to the edge of the lake and left us at a flattened off rocky bank that was suitable for our improvised camping spot.

Morning came, after my mattress lost its air. There seemed to be an unwritten law that my mattress was supposed to leak, because it always did. My husband went down the rocky bank to see if he could discover the problem with the motor. Our little camp fire was burning nicely and I could fix breakfast. I had been sitting on some folded towels by the side of the picnic basket and I got up and moved the basket closer to the fire. Then my eyes caught sight of the coiled up rattlesnake that was moving out from where the picnic basket had been.

Doing what would be expected of a woman I screamed a loud terrifying scream. My husband was equally frightened, he was sure whatever the problem it was too late to save me. He and the dog both rushed to my side and the dog wanted to attack the snake but I held him back. Things were put in order, we had a nice breakfast and were able to send a message by a passing boater to a friend to come and get us and tow us to the nearest dock.

The snakes enjoyed the lake too. They could be seen swimming in the water near the shore.

Ghostly Happenings

It has been reasonably quiet about ghosts annoying people in their homes. I am used to hearing rattling and thumping, and occasionally something hits the Indian drum a big whack to get my attention. Others who are not familiar with ghosts sometimes ask me for help to discuss the problem and try to find a cure.

An acquaintance who contacted me previously said he thought the ghosts had come back. He heard noises at night that kept him awake. My Spirit Guide reported that indeed the ghosts returned.

My Spirit Guide said he would remove them, and the person later reported a couple of quiet nights. I hope the ghosts are not persistent and come back again. If they do we will throw them out again. I am always happy to help someone with their ghost problems.

A few months ago I had several requests in a row, mostly from young people with children who were concerned about the strange things going on in their houses. One by one my Spirit Guide removed them.

In one case the earth bound spirit was helped to another plane to be with other family spirits. The young man was killed while he was bicycling with a friend and was hit by a drunk driver. For many years the spirit of the young man haunted his cousin. She would come home to find her husband's shoes in the middle of the living room, and other items moved around the house. The spirit sent icy chills down his cousin's arms with his touch.

One morning the cousin's daughter spent the night and was asleep on a couch in the living room. These are her words: "It was in the late hours of the morning. I was lying on the couch when I heard the door to Mom's room open, announced by the noise of several necklaces hanging on the door knob. I looked over to the hallway expecting to see Mom shuffling into view, but I saw a man instead. I was surprised to see a visitor coming from her room but it didn't frighten me at all. My uncle Harlan was sleeping in the guest room and Mom did not come out of her room. I watched the man glide to the rocker in the living room and sit down. He looked young, not tall and thin, not short and stocky, but well fit. His hair was short, dark and straight. Then I heard a dog lapping up water. At that point I thought perhaps Harlan had brought his dog, Cleo, down from my grandmother's house to spend the night, even though I had not seen or heard any signs of his large dog being here.

Then the visitor got up from the chair and walked my way. Thinking he would use the computer, I just covered my head so he wouldn't see how messy I looked and I did not want to meet anyone when I looked so unkempt. (Vanity, you know!) I didn't hear anything after that. The sliding glass doors did not open, and he did not walk back into my view. He wore dark clothes; a long sleeved tight fitting shirt the same color as the pants. He was solid although I couldn't see any reflection from his skin or clothes and I did not see his face at all. His presence didn't scare me and he didn't give off any negative vibes."

With the help of Spirit Guides this young man's spirit was able to cross over to another plane.

I will sit patiently by like the repair man in the appliance commercial who never had any work to do because his product was so well made and long lasting.

Come on, ghosties!

Practical Jokes

There always seemed to be a contest in my family to see who could pull the best joke on another family member. It wasn't always the children; sometimes the parents became involved along with the others.

I'll start with the bean patch. My daughter and her husband lived next door within shouting distance from our house. A reasonably flat spot that could be reached by the water hose lay between our places and we decided to fence it and plant a garden.

Metal posts were set and a six foot high wire fence was put in place. The ground was prepared and our spot was ready to plant the eagerly awaited garden. Since we have an abundance of deer around our area we had to make certain that the fence was high enough to keep them out of our garden.

Spring came and the weather was just right to start planting the seeds. We watched every day to see if any sprouts were showing above the ground. Some of us were guilty of digging down to see what was taking place with the seeds in the earth and it was wonderful to finally see the results beginning to show.

We pampered the little plants with pride, thinking about the results when we could start harvesting the nice fresh vegetables and canning them in the pressure cooker. We could almost see them grow in the warm sun.

The weeds were a problem in the new ground and we worked feverishly keeping them under control.

It was beautiful to behold the corn stalks sticking up in the air above the luscious tomato vines, green pepper plants, cabbage plants, and huge squash vines. The bean vines were growing rapidly and climbed the wires we had in place to hold them up. Soon they had blossoms and then the nice tender green beans were almost ready to pick.

Since my husband and I had been victimized in the practical joke routine in our family we decided this was a great opportunity to get even. We could make it look like the deer had been in the garden. The split end of a pine limb made a perfect deer track in the soft ground. A smaller limb was found and split to make the fawn's track. Everything was in order. I even pulled some leaves off the vines to make look like they had been eaten by the doe. The set up was perfect. Nothing had been overlooked for our farce.

The next morning there was a frantic telephone call from our daughter. The deer had been in the garden. Of course we said "Oh no, they can't get over that fence." She would not take no for an answer. The little track was there too. But how did the little track get in there, the wire was too tight for even a rabbit to get through. We dropped the subject for a while and let them think about the situation. Finally another phone call reported they were going to town to get more wire to put on top of the fence. At that point we thought the joke had gone far enough. It was a thirty mile trip to town and the extra rolls of wire would have been costly, to say nothing of the time involved. We had to come clean and confess our sin.

We had a hard time convincing them that it was a joke: the evidence was there, the torn bean vines and the tracks in the damp earth. We smiled, knowing that sooner or later they would get even.

THE CHICKEN AND THE EGG

No creature is safe in the land of practical jokes, not even a little resin hen sitting in a basket with a nest full of eggs showing under her feathers. I found it in my back yard hiding in the creeping myrtle around the outdoor fountain. My youngest daughter was playing a trick on me and I recognized it immediately. The little hen looked so real with the little eggs poking out from under her feathers; it was hard to believe I was being tricked.

My son has some acres of land bordering ours. It is a cool, shady wooded area with mossy rocks and ferns, a place where he finds solitude and enjoys the togetherness he finds with nature. He walks through the woods and can look down on a creek that is barely seen behind the screen of maple trees and berry bushes. A magnificent yellow pine tree stands tall and straight near the creek bank. Timber fallers visualize several thousand feet of very fine lumber standing there. It is treasure, never to be touched with axe and saw.

I started thinking about the little chicken in a basket, how nice she would look partly hidden from view under a bush on his little corner of land. I would not hide her completely, just enough that the white feathers would attract his attention. I did it.

In a few days he came to visit, and just as predicted he went for a walk to his acreage in the woods. I have many laughs thinking of how it must have been: he saw something that was different. What could it be? He looked closer. It looked like a chicken sitting on a nest. She was sitting very still. He walked up to her slowly not wanting to scare her off the nest. He got closer and closer and picked up a stick to touch her with. She just set there like a rock hen.

Then he knew. He had been tricked! He gathered her up still sitting in the basket with the eggs poking out around her feathers and walked back home. I will always cherish that moment, that funny grin when he handed her to me. "Well done," I thought to myself.

The little hen had paid for her keep in the amusement she had brought to us so I decided to place her on the front deck among the many house plants. I thought it would be a safe place but I was wrong. The raccoons took the eggs one at a time until they were all gone. They must have thought they were real or at least something to play with. I haven't decided how to replace the artificial eggs for a resin chicken. I may have to make them out of potter's clay or plaster of Paris and then bolt them down. Maybe she will have to endure the empty nest syndrome that happens to people.

THE RAT AND ITS AMAZING TRAVELS

My daughter and I enjoy house-sitting at my son's place while he is away from home for a few days. There is a spring that comes out of the mountain side behind his place and is the beginning of a little stream that flows past his house. It has a little water fall along the way and a trail that goes into the woods, an ideal place for a walk to enjoy the peace and quiet.

There is competition between the siblings to see who can come up with the best tricks to play on the other. Usually I get to be the observer, but sometimes I too get caught up in the mischief.

One day while she was shopping my daughter found a life size rubber rat which she kept in her suitcase until the time was right to give her brother a good fright. House sitting while he was gone created a perfect time. She put the rat in his shower which was usually not well lit. Getting ready for work in the morning is a hasty routine for him.

When the shower was turned on the dark colored rat performed beautifully, spinning and whirling around in the white bottom of the shower. Of course we missed the show but the way it was described gave us the amusement we hoped for. Trying to keep away from such an object in the shower was a great dance routine. He never considered that it could be a rubber object placed to get even for some prior prank.

The rat was his to do with as he pleased, and he had plans.

THE RAT GOES CAMPING

This is my son's version of the rat incident which he wrote in a story about a hunting trip in which a group of hunters packed in from the trail head with pack mules. I asked him for permission to use it in my book:

"The rat was well traveled. It had "Made in China" on his belly, was made of rubber and must have come to America on a ship. My younger sister found him in Jackson County, Oregon, and somehow he came to Douglas County, thanks to her, and ended up in my shower. It was there that I met him lurking in a corner and as the water hit him when I turned on the shower he spun across the white plastic floor of the shower stall. Scared me, or at least startled me enough to jump back. Then it made its way to my dental office where it was tied to the leg of a dental receptionist's chair. As the chair was pulled out the rat was activated and caused some jumping and yelling by the lady. Then Mike Sutch called to borrow some packing boxes for a mule packing trip to the Idaho Gospel Hump Wilderness Area. She intervened and taped the rat to the inside of the packing box lid so it would jump out at Mike when he opened the lid, and it worked well. He jumped. When the gear was unpacked the rat found its way into Mike's Uncle Ed's sleeping bag. We thought this was the end of the rat story, but not.

Enter the real rat. About the third night of our hunting trip I awoke at 2:30 A.M. I awoke to the sound of tiny toe nails scratching on the plastic tarp we used as a tent floor. I turned on my flashlight and its beam revealed a live rat, and a big one. About a one pound wood rat was dragging a piece of tamarack kindling across the floor, and he took it under Mike's cot over in the corner of the tent. Soon he was back and had a bigger piece of wood, was intent on building his nest for the winter under the beds, and thought he had just struck it rich with a nice warm dry shelter, with lots of peanuts and food scraps to eat. He even pulled Mike's wool cap into position for the liner. About then I yelled at Mike, waking him up and telling him that a big rat was setting up housekeeping under his bed. He thought I was responsible and had a string tied on the rubber rat and was pulling it across the floor to pester him. Just then as he was looking under the bed with his flashlight the real rat jumped up eye ball to eye ball with Mike, on his sleeping bed and then jumped over to my bed. Finally Mike was convinced that it was a real live wood rat and he got under the cot and reclaimed his hat and tossed out the fire wood. That was the last we saw of the live rat but the rubber rat is still a threat to reappear."

Skeletons in the family closet

An author and historian in my area published many books on the history of the settling of the country. I am amazed at the research she did on each family and piece of land. It is very thorough and she tells it like it was and holds no punches.

I appreciate very much being able to borrow these family tid-bits from the writings of Barbara Hegne, entitled Yonder Hills. I had the pleasure of meeting the lady and our paths crossed several times when we were restoring and repairing old books. She is the curator of a local museum.

My own family is among those she has written about in her books. It was an education to me learning about my family in the early days. I would never have known that a new school house had to be built because the snow had broken down the original one. My father and all of his siblings went to that school. Most of them stayed in school long enough to learn the basics that were necessary. They all learned to read well and had good legible hand writing.

The author tells about an incident that took place with my paternal grandmother. It seems like her father-in-law stayed at her place and the arrangement was not always pleasant. It appears that there was much friction between the two. I remember my grandmother who passed away in

1936. She was a good grandma and I remember staying at her place when I was very small. She was very important to us and we loved her dearly.

There was an epidemic of typhoid fever in the early 1900's and several of my family members were lost to it, including my grandfather. My great grandfather died in 1889 and my grandfather died in 1904. After my grandfather's death my grandmother started seeing the spirit of her father-in-law hanging around the place. It scared her very badly.

One evening she was late getting home with her children and she was afraid to go home. She stopped by the next door neighbors and asked them to accompany her. When they arrived they found the kerosene lamp lit and no one around. After searching the house for ghosts of the old man they and reminded her if she had been a little nicer to him he probably would have left her alone.

Daddy's old Fiddle

The picture I have of my father when he was a young man shows me a fair skinned blue eyed person. That never changed. I could see kindness in his face, a love of music, fun and dancing. That didn't change either. I was never able to learn much about the genealogy, but the names and appearances made me think of England, Scotland and Ireland.

My great grandfather and grandmother left Missouri on a wagon train. My great grandmother is buried somewhere along the Oregon Trail and my great grandfather arrived in Jacksonville, Oregon in 1852. Different family members have studied the genealogy but it doesn't seem to get back past a certain point in time.

My father learned to read music when he took a correspondence course. He mostly played the old time fiddle and that was always done by ear. He played many tunes, from the popular square dances of the time to dreamy waltzes.

People held dances in their homes and the music was supplied by anyone who could play an instrument. The music was played for the two step, waltzes, schottische, quadrilles, polkas, and probably some I have forgotten. My father played them all. As an added attraction he could dance the Irish jig which was done like tap dancing.

He could play the spoons. That act originated in Ireland as playing the bones. A pair of sheep ribs was held together between the fingers and the hand and created a rhythm when struck on the knee by the other hand. The spoons are played by placing the spoons together with the conclave facing out with the fingers between the handles to space them. The spoons are struck against the knee with the hand to make a rhythm. I always remember what a treat it was when he played the spoons to amuse the family.

The dances lasted all night and the children were put on a bed crosswise and covered with all the coats that were available.

At one of the dances there was a mishap. A lady sat on my father's fiddle and broke the top. He missed it terribly until one winter he had prepared a slab of red fir and carved a new top for his broken fiddle. The only tools he had was a hand saw and a pocket knife. He spent many hours working on it. He ordered clamps and glue and anything he needed from a catalog. With no sand paper to finish the surface, he used a piece of broken glass. When his hand carved top was completed it had a beautiful tone and he played it for many years afterward.

It became mine when he could no longer play it. My oldest brother made a wooden case with a glass top to display it and my daddy's old fiddle hangs on my wall. It is one of my proudest possessions.

Scaredy Cat

Since I was the only girl in in the middle of the group of five boys, I had an interesting childhood. My older brothers had their own rifles and hunted wild game while I was a little girl.

They knew every trail leading to the mountains and occasionally it was dark when they came home, often carrying the results of the hunting trip on their back. They used the flash light only to find the trail to home when they could no longer see it.

Often they knew they were being followed by a cougar or other wild animal. I was always amazed when they told about their experiences when we were all sitting around the wood heater after the evening meal. In those days the noon meal was called dinner and the evening meal was called supper.

I was never a brave one, always afraid of the dark. Things haven't changed much, I am still afraid in the dark. Strange noises in the woods often started me for home looking over my shoulder so see if something was following me. I am glad that if one of us was going to be a scaredy cat that I was the chosen one. It was better for it to be the girl in the family than one of the brothers. That would have been very hard for them to live down, coming from a pioneer family of mountaineers.

When I was a child my family lived on a quarter of a section of land, or one hundred and sixty acres. It was mostly woods and forest until my father cleared the land to plant a field and a place for the home site with a garden and out buildings. A few hundred yards from our log house there was a spring that came from under an alder tree and made a little stream that ran down into a canyon below. It was one of my favorite places where I would often go and sit by the spring and watch a couple of little fish my brothers had put in it. It was a peaceful and quiet place but sometimes I would hear something crashing around in the dense woods. Even though I was sure the noise was a deer I would be terrified and go back home. I was less frightened when I was older but never really brave.

Wild violets grew around the banks and it was my little piece of Heaven. It is one of my secret things that give me pleasure when I need to count my blessings.

DEVIL IN THE CLASS ROOM

As we travel down life's path we have lots of time to review the things we should have done and the things we did that we wish we had done differently. That brings to mind an incident that took place when I was a senior in high school.

I cannot remember why the class became unruly during our literature class. We had a nice teacher who was in her first year of teaching. For some reason the whole class started throwing verbal darts at the teacher. Everyone in the class took a jab at her, except for one nice boy who took her part.

I really do not know why we acted up in class that day. I'm sure there must have been some nice students there but it didn't show up in our actions. The only thing I can think of after all those years this that it was Shakespeare's fault. We were all struggling with final exams and I suppose that was our way of letting off steam.

When I attended our fifty year class reunion nearly everyone there brought up that day when we were all so terrible. Every one of us admitted feeling remorse about the incident. The teacher should have sent the whole class to the principal's office but instead, she laid her head on her desk and cried.

We didn't get off Scott free. Everyone one of us paid for our actions and probably will until the day we die. My spirit Guide tells me she hears me and forgives.

School Bullies

We read about it in the news nearly every day. It is not something new. Bullying probably has been going on since time began. The cave men were no doubt equally guilty and their writings scrawled on the cave walls might be telling us about it.

My husband lost his father when he was nine years old, and being small for his age made him an easy target for bullies. Fortunately his father had taught him some valuable lessons about survival and trust. It reminds me of the song, "A boy named Sue."

His mother was not able to be there all the time to protect him and work to feed her little boy and his sister, so the lessons in self-preservation came in handy many times. In doing so it caused him to grow up untrusting and ready to fight at the drop of a hat.

When our own children were in high school a young lady close to our family was the subject of bullying by a gang of girls at school. She tried to handle it herself until the situation became so flammable the young lady had to confide in her parents. She was threatened with bodily harm and she was afraid to go to school. It was then her parents discovered her problem; someone had to escort her to class because a gang of girls threatened her.

The day that she had to tell her parents about her problem the gang leader called her at home and thought she was talking to the young lady, but the father listened to the phone call and could see that there was a bad situation that needed to be taken care of immediately.

He took his daughter to school and a meeting was held with the principal, the leader of the gang of girls and her mother. It was a very intense meeting. Mostly the principal sat and listened with his mouth open but saying nothing. It was evident that he was shocked by the bullying that was happening without his knowledge. The mother tried to defend her daughter but the evidence was well stacked against her. Her denial did not hold up.

The father handled it in his own way and the principal said he had never heard anyone talk like that. He told the young lady that if she ever did anything to harm his daughter that he would take her home at the end of his belt, the buckle end. Every step of the way he would tear hunks out of her fanny that would lay quivering on the sidewalk. The girl said she would have her boy friend handle him, and the mother said she would have her husband get in the act and take care of him. Neither of them showed up.

Whatever happened in the principal's office that day seemed to stop the bullying, at least in that instance. The terrified student was able to walk down the halls to class without an escort the rest of the year.

Times have changed. That incident took place about fifty years ago. Now the bullied girl's father would be the villain and probably be arrested for abusing the abuser.

Rings with legs

Rings have a way of walking away if left unattended and fall into the view of some people who like pretty shiny things. With vehicles it is called "joy riding."

Since I worked most of the time it was easy to need assistance with household chores and yard work. At the same time I felt like I was doing a good deed by giving the young people in the area a chance to make a little money. They were nice and likable neighbors and easy to trust.

The ring that came up missing was not an everyday possession but a family heirloom that my mother had given to me. I cherished it the same way my mother did. It was said to be an engagement ring of someone in past generations, and was a very interesting design with two emeralds surrounded with moon stones.

My mother's desires were very few. She was content with the basics and simple country life. If something special should come her way she found more enjoyment from it by giving it away. The two things that she cherished and guarded carefully were the ring that was handed down to her and her autograph book from her school days that were given to her by her parents.

When my young neighbor girl helped me with vacuuming and dusting one day I noticed that the cherished ring was gone from a tray in a dresser drawer. I knew I had to be very tactful and not make any accusations or it would be gone forever. I decided to get her help in some detective work; I would ask her to help me find it.

I called her on the telephone and in a pitiful voice I told her I had lost something and I wondered if she could help me look for it. She came immediately and when I answered the door I couldn't help but see the worried and frightened look in her eyes. She asked what it was and I explained about the ring being so dear to me and how sad I was that I had misplaced it. I asked her if she would look around the dresser and in the drawer and see if she could find it. She was gone about a minute or two and came out of the bedroom with the ring in the palm of her hand. "Is this what you are looking for," she asked.

I thanked her over and over and asked where she found it. She told me it was back in the corner of the drawer. I had already looked there and I knew it was not so. I had the ring back in my possession and she had saved face. We were both happy with the situation. The matter was put to rest and we remained friends. She graduated from school, married and had a baby boy. We kept in touch for several years. There had been trauma in her life and I fully understood that she had a need to uplift her spirits. I think it was a good lesson for both of us; she learned humility and learned about understanding.

So much for rings walking.

ANOTHER RING WALKING

"Stolen" doesn't have a good ring to it. I prefer to use "A plan gone bad." It happened when a very young man was doing some work around my house. After the small amount of yard work was completed there were a couple of inside chores that I wanted his help with so I asked him to come inside and showed him what I needed done.

After he left I missed a gold ring that I had planned to take to the jeweler to have a stone tightened on it. It was a gift to my husband from me and something that was very dear to his heart. I knew I had to act quickly and thoughtfully to get the ring back in my possession before my husband returned from work and missed it.

The young man was living with his grandmother and I thought she would understand my predicament. I knew where she lived, in a small house several miles up on a mountain road that was not much more than a wagon track. It was a very hot day, 106*. The brush growing on the bank scratched the car but I did not allow that or the extreme heat to be an impediment.

When I reached the little house the grandmother come outside to talk to me. I told her that her grandson had taken the ring and I had to get it back before my husband came home and missed it. I told her I didn't want to cause trouble for the boy; I just wanted the ring back. A young lady that lived at the place asked if she could ride back to town with me. She explained to me that her people were not the only ones that stole things. I had to agree and we parted on friendly terms.

After dark that same evening I heard a knock on the door. It was a nice looking young man with a stern look in his eyes. His first words were "I hear you are accusing my nephew of stealing a ring." I knew immediately the matter needed to be settled tactfully, once and for all. I invited him inside and asked him to have a chair. He asked why I thought his nephew had taken it. My explanation was that he had been the only one in the house. He asked if it was possible that someone else could have come in through the window and taken it. I realized I had to be resourceful, so I said yes, it was possible.

That was what it took, a slight hint that his nephew could be innocent. He handed me a small brown bag which I opened and much to my amazement was my husband's gold ring in the bottom of it. He explained that he saw something shining in the gutter and picked it up and it was the ring. When he heard that I was missing a ring he wanted to return it to me. I thanked him though my tears and told him how nice it was that he brought it to me.

It was a happy ending. The boy didn't get in trouble, the uncle did a good deed and made him feel good about the situation and I could sleep well that night. I took the ring to the jeweler and had the repair completed before I told my husband about the incident.

THE SPIRIT OF AN INDIAN CHIEF

When my husband was a young boy his mother and some of her friends had been checking their genealogies and she came home enthused with the discovery that she was a direct descendent of a famous Indian Chief. At that particular time in my husband's life he was not much in interested in her findings and being a normal boy he ridiculed the whole idea.

In later years he became interested in his heritage and wanted to learn more about his mother's findings. Learning about the Chief's life was not a problem but he could find nothing in the records about the Chief's wife, who was his great grandmother.

My husband's grandmother was married to a German who did not want the subject of heritage discussed and forbade it to be a topic of conversation. His grandmother had a mind of her own and was not easily stifled about the subject. She was proud of her heritage and stood her ground.

Out of curiosity one day I asked through my Spirit Guide if I could communicate with the Chief's spirit. Much to my surprise I was told his spirit was here. We had a nice conversation and he said that my husband was a fine man and he would have been welcome in the tribe.

I asked him if he could tell me about my husband's great grandmother. He said she had suffered a head injury from a bullet and was not able to keep up her duties in the tribe. The women were the ones that did most of the work around the camp and the men were the hunters that provided food.

A German trader came to the camp with blankets and other things that were needed by the tribe. The injured Indian wife, who was pregnant, was traded to the German trader. The child was my husband's grandmother.

The Chief's spirit gave me names of other family members that we recognized. He told me through the spirits that he liked my hair. He said I was a palomino. He told me that if I needed him he would be here.

The Chief's spirit goes to the mountains when my son is hunting and tries to show him where the elk herds can be found and sees to the hunter's safety. It was a wonderful experience to communicate with the spirit of a famous Indian Chief who was my late husband's great grandfather.

Are we fair to ourselves?

As we get older and look back on our lives, it seems natural that we make some changes in our approach to things. We think about things we said to people, perhaps in jest that ended up being hurtful instead of funny. We think of the times when we were rude, even though it was not intentional that we wish we could do over.

In later years we think about decisions we made and we wish we had done lots of things differently. I feel better hearing my Spirit guide tell me through my dowsing pendulum and alphabetical chart that we are judged by what we are today, not what we were in the past. Our thoughts and regrets are all taken care of through our desire to make things right.

We can secretly send our apologies back through the past and they will be heard and accepted. All is not lost. The circumstances at the time dictated what we did and how we handled situations. What seemed right and proper at the time may look different to us now.

Perhaps that is the way life was meant to be. We were given time to fix things and make us feel better. We are told that we should forgive and forget. I have a problem with that. I do not forgive easily and my memory serves me well. The problem comes when I try to add new knowledge to the brain that was taught by the three "Rs"; that is the basic reading, writing and arithmetic.

Electronics does not come easily. Fortunately there is good help available.

I seem to find comfort in analyzing life and coming up with the theory that I am a better person today because of past lessons.

Apologies

The theories that I share in this chapter will no doubt be controversial. Sharing is what writing is all about. It is an exchange of ideas which are often objectionable to others. Otherwise our thoughts would be kept to ourselves, and sometimes they can be useful.

The subject of apologies comes to mind. When Junior bops his little cousin on the head with a stuffed animal and there is loud wailing, often the parents step in to settle the conflict. Sometimes Junior is made to apologize to his little cousin, regardless of the adage of being innocent until proven guilty. That is where my theory begins.

It appears to me that it is unfair to insist that an apology be made. Junior probably isn't sorry and to make him say otherwise is an injustice, compelling him to be dishonest in his evaluations of himself.

Often in the news we read where a comedian or other notable character says something objectionable and gets in trouble with all the powers involved. We read where they apologize like Junior is forced to do or they will be in big trouble. I question the sincerity of the public apology being forced by political "do gooders". I would prefer to hear the person say," That was not wise and I should have phrased it differently." To be forced into making a public apology to me is empty and meaningless as well as dishonest.

There are times when I can see the need of saying "I'm sorry." If I turn around suddenly and knock someone off their feet, I am really sorry. It pops out of my mouth automatically. That is an honest apology with no forethought. If someone insists on an apology it has no meaning.

A fellow I read about named Shakespeare used this phrase in one of his tragedies. "To Thine own self be true." Good thinking.

METAL ALLERGIES

It happened on my wrist when I put my watch on and wore it for a few hours. There was a black and blue spot just the size of the watch on my wrist when I took the watch off. "I'll fix that," I said to myself. I covered the back of the watch with leather, all except the knob on the end that sets the time. I wore it again and a red, burned looking spot appeared where the knob was touching my skin. "I'll fix that," I said again. My fix was to start carrying it in my purse.

That incident caused me to be more aware when the skin started acting like a sun burn and started flaking off around my ears where the metal in the frames of my eye glasses touched my face. "I'll fix that" I said to myself.

I told others about my problem and it was suggested that I cover the metal with nail polish. That sounded reasonable and I did that. I think it helped a little.

That wasn't enough. I decided to cover the frames with tape but the only thing around was some band aids, so I cut the sticky ends off and tried to cover the glasses with it; not too satisfactory. The stiffness in the material was enough to make a rough, uneven padding. Then I tried some adhesive tape that is used on bandages and that was even less acceptable for the smooth covering I was seeking.

Each time I tried something different I had a struggle getting the tape off the metal frames until I remembered reading about the merits of WD 40. When I sprayed it on, presto! The tape came off immediately.

In the meantime I discovered that the plastic covered curve that goes over and behind the ears was still causing skin problems. It needed to be covered as well. My next experiment was with an adhesive mole skin material found at the foot care section at the store. It was flexible and soft and by cutting it in strips about one fourth of an inch wide it worked very well by wrapping it around and around until the entire metal frame was covered. The plastic frame around the lens does not seem to be a problem.

I am not aware of how other people handle the problem with the metal in the eye glass frames. When I have my next check up with my Ophthalmologist I will discuss the problem and see if he has answers. I suppose if they are carved out of wood that might pose problems too.

In the meantime my glasses are not very scenic, but comfort is more desirable than vanity at this stage in my life. "The better to see you, my dear."

Missing wheat flakes

This is such a strange thing that happened I almost hesitate to write about it. Some people might think their intelligence was being compromised.

For a beginning, I have many food allergies that I have learned to deal with, either by ignoring or avoiding them. Sometimes I have to prove to myself that the food is really the culprit and in doing so I have more than one upset before being willing to give it up.

By the end of the day this body gets weary and it is easy to have a snack of something light and quick. Most of the time it seems satisfying to have a dish of cold cereal and fruit and there are no obvious signs of nutrition being abused.

So it was with my recent evening snack, even though there were suspicions that the wheat might be causing allergies or perhaps all the additives were not appreciated by my inner self. I went to bed and in a while I awoke very ill and nauseated. I asked my Spirit Guide through my dowsing pendulum and alphabetical chart if he could tell me what I should do about the upset stomach. His answer was to take a large spoon full of honey. I did that and it helped immediately.

The next day I planned to put tape on the box of cereal and give it to someone without problems. When I went to get it, it was not to be found. I looked the house over and searched every cupboard where I might have inadvertently put it. I then asked my Spirit Guide if he could tell me where it was. The answer was yes, the spirits threw it out for the animals because it was not good for anyone to eat it. He told me that it was toxic to my body and could even be fatal.

There you have it, as strange as it seems. I still keep looking and scratching my head. The spirits have their own way of handling things.

SPIRIT THINGS

This book has many subjects; some are about wild life and practical jokes people have pulled on others. There is a chapter here and there about spiritual things that have happened through my connection with the other side. Eventually it will have to be organized but for now I will keep on truckin'. I will sort it out later.

Since life is a learning experience, many things come to mind that we can share with others. I do not permit myself the luxury of being morbid and sad. Obviously my frame of mind doesn't just affect myself, but can make the days of those around me happy or sad. The object of my writing is to bring sunshine into the lives of others. Come on, sunshine!

Through the years I kept in touch with a high school friend. We would meet at the grocery store usually by accident and chat for a few minutes, mostly about this or that person we remembered at school. I remembered her being laughing and friendly and well-liked by the others.

Her husband passed away and we shared the troubled times. I lost my husband also and we shared.

One of her daughters lived at home and was her mother's care person. She sent an e-mail to let me know when her mother was ill and I responded to keep in touch. Occasionally I would get a hand written note from my friend. She told me that she had fallen and injured her head. Again I heard through the daughter's e-mail that her mother was in the hospital with pneumonia. Several illnesses took place and one day I saw my friend's obituary in the newspaper. Shortly after that I got a hand written note from her daughter telling me that my friend had passed away.

The daughter and I kept in touch. She had a history of illnesses. Everything that could happen to a person happened to her. I had the feeling that she was a hypochondriac but I could see the evidence to show that she really had been very ill. She had one illness after the other. She would e-mail me to say she was going into the hospital. She would e-mail me when she was home again.

The last time she went to the hospital I kept waiting to hear from her and after a few days I learned that she was in intensive care and her condition was extreme. Then I saw the obituary in the paper. I thought after a few days her spirit would contact me but I heard nothing from the spirits. Finally I got a short message and she wanted to thank me for being her friend.

It was then my spirit guide told me through my dowsing pendulum and alphabetical chart that her spirit was not coming back. It had been sent to the place where bad people go. Then I learned the reason her mother fell and injured her head was because her daughter had hit her on the head with a broom handle and knocked her down.

At that point I could see many things. I could see why she told me that other family members were avoiding her. I could see there were very bad spirits surrounding her and causing her life to be one of illness and turmoil. I tried to find out from my spirit guide where the bad spirits came from. He says it is best to let it be. It was because of evil thoughts that had abounded in the area.

My experience with the people in that household added weight to my belief that mean, bad people pay for their deeds down the road. I look back in life and see that some of the people I knew who had done things that damaged others had bad things happen to them. It reminds me of an old saying, "Those who dance must pay the fiddler".

The Subject of Exorcisms

Exorcism is a topic of interest to me but I never had occasion to look into it closely. My research about it gave me conflicting opinions and I came away empty handed.

An acquaintance of mine told me that when she was extremely ill and unable to think for herself she was a completely different person when she regained her consciousness. Some Archaic spirits from an unknown religion had taken over her mind. I met her after her illness but it was obvious to me that she had been taken over by another power.

When I read about the subject and someone says it doesn't happen, and I read another opinion quite the opposite I am left with conflicting thoughts. It is times like that when I ask my Spirit Guide for information and advice. This is what he tells me: "It is true that a person in a weakened condition can be taken over by bad spirits. They can be removed easily by the Spirit Guide and it is not necessary to have a big exorcist production to make it happen. It doesn't take a high priest or special intelligence to do it."

It is very helpful to a person to learn about pendulum dowsing and reading the alphabetical chart that spells out messages and answers to questions that might arise. It puts a person in touch with their Spirit Guide to remove unwanted spirits from a residence no matter how far away the problem is. My Guide removed ghosts from my granddaughter's house on the other side of our continent and several from houses several hundred miles away.

I have known some very mean people in my lifetime and now I look back and wonder if they were possessed by a mean spirit. If I had known about Spirit Guides earlier in my life I could possibly have had the assistance to rid the person of their ordeal. Surely people don't choose to be mean and hurtful to others.

Vocal Spirits and strange lights

It is seldom that I hear voices from the spirits. Shortly after my husband passed away I was sitting in my chair one evening half asleep when I heard his voice say, "coffee." I checked with my spirit guide through my dowsing pendulum and alphabetical chart to see what the meaning of it was. He wanted me to fix the coffee pot so it would be ready in the morning.

When I was going to school and living away from home I heard my mother's voice call my name. It happened several times. It was coming from her live spirit. I have heard my children's voices also. I have heard my daughter's voice at the door but she was not there.

Another strange phenomenal occurrence has me wondering. Some lights appear on the walls of my bedroom. They appear so briefly and leave before I have a chance to evaluate the cause. It is like a flashlight being turned on and off very quickly. It has shown on the wall paneling in about a four foot area and one time there was a bright round light about ten inches in diameter shining on the floor behind the bed room door. Another time I saw a bright red round light about the size of a dime shining on the wall by the side of the bedroom door.

My Spirit Guide says we are being spied on. By whom? Why? I wish I had the answer for it.

HAUNTED RENTAL HOUSE

A couple in New Jersey are having problems with strange noises in their rented house. They hear footsteps and door slamming and have had something tugging on their blankets. They are terrified and want their rental deposit returned so they can move to a different house. Their landlord denies the house is haunted and thinks the people are just trying to get out of paying the rent.

My psychic and spiritual abilities have led me to similar situations where I have been able to remove the ghosts through my Spirit Guide by remote control. The two previous books I authored have several chapters of e-mail conversations in which frightened people hear strange noises and things happening in their houses. It is not their imagination and they are very much relieved to find that I really can get the ghosts to move on.

The ghosts that move into peoples' houses are earthbound spirits that lost their lives suddenly and they did not have assistance to find the gates of Heaven where they must wait and rest until taken inside. Sometimes they will leave if they are asked to, but it often takes some help from Spirit Guides to get them to move on. Professional ghost busters try to remove them. I am not sure what that entails but my Spirit Guide has been very successful and clearing the houses of ghosts. I am able to learn who they are and how they lost their lives. A few times they are reluctant to leave and my Guide sends for help. A few times they returned and have to be removed again.

There are people who have the ability to assist the earthbound spirits to find the way. It is often referred to as "finding the light." The spirit of a family member was recently helped to the other side. His spirit was seen and heard for many years by more than one person.

It is understandable that there are non-believers. That is their right and their privilege. Sometimes people don't understand about a subject until they come face to face with it. After I learned about pendulum dowsing and being able to communicate with the other side through my alphabetical chart I learned about the Spirit Guides that are there to protect and assist us. They are very helpful in my life.

Each of my publications has a chapter that tells how to make dowsing pendulums, how to learn to dowse and read the chart that spells out messages from the other side by swinging to the letters. A copy of such a chart is included in each book.

Learning to repair books

My oldest brother had many interests that sometimes caused conflicts because he could not be two places at the same time. That is where I came in. He and his wife owned an antique store and the overflow required a second business in town which was mostly old and out of print books.

He also had a shop with tools for working with wood and a lot of the time he asked me to mind the store. His time was always at a premium. He was an outdoors person and enjoyed collecting antique guns and other items.

In my time at his book store I developed an interest in the condition of the books and learned people's interests. I took books off the shelf and looked at the loose pages and torn covers and wonder what I could do to make them more presentable and saleable.

My husband was a very literary person and when he was in school he was a very good reader. His literature teacher would ask him to read in front of the class. Shakespeare was one of his favorite studies and he never tired of telling me about different plays that were discussed. Unfortunately I never became a fan of the classics.

When I found a large volume of the complete works of Shakespeare I decided to see if I could improve its appearance and make it readable. It was just a hulk with no covers, a real challenge.

I had never paid any attention to how a book was put together. I didn't know what held the pages together to make a book, I didn't know it had hinges to hold it in the covers and how they were used to fasten it in between the boards. The only thing I was sure of was that it was a real mess and needed a lot of help to make it saleable and readable.

I purchased the hulk and took it home with me. I practiced on it to give it to my husband. I knew he would like it regardless of the outcome. One of my hobbies was leather craft and I bought some tooling leather and carved the title into the cover. It was very stiff but it turned out beautifully. Somehow I was able to hold the pages in the stiff piece of leather. It was very unprofessional, but there was no one else in the area to ask for help. If I was going to be able to repair books I would have to teach myself.

About the time I became interested in repairing books we moved to another state. I could see how the books were put together and that sometimes I could use the original covers. I was motivated by the fact that there were a lot of books that needed repairing and no one was doing it. I put an ad in the newspaper and was surprised at the calls I received. I had so much to learn and no one to ask for help. Eventually I discovered thin leather for the covers and if gold printing was needed I could take it to a printer to get it done. I blundered through and used each book as a learning experience. No one complained, they didn't know how either.

Eventually my husband retired and we ended back in our home state. He became involved in helping me with the repairing of the books and could see things that needed to be done differently. Together we learned how to put the stitching in the spine of the books and the process went much faster and better. We obtained a hot press and my husband was able to put the gold printing on the new covers. The time he served as a printers apprentice came in very handy.

We were contacted by the local newspaper and the reporter wrote a full page article about the work we were doing with pictures of us surrounded with the books we were repairing. It was sent by Associated Press all over the country and was read by many people that sent us books to repair from many different states. We received a large box of children's books that took us most of the summer to complete.

Book repair was a lucrative and enjoyable hobby where we met many interesting people. Others wanted us to teach them how to do it but after what we had gone through to learn it I was saving it like an old family recipe. When we retired from it one of my granddaughters was eager to learn the skill and take over where we left off.

We did relent a little and made a two hour video tape showing everything we did and what materials were needed. Mostly they were purchased by book dealers that wanted to improve their books for sale. We ended up with some DVDs as we progressed electronically.

That was an interesting episode in our lives. There was so much to learn.

Snow birds

It all started with flea markets. My husband and I heard of a giant flea market in Arizona where people all over the country gather in the winters and mix business and pleasure. It started out as a huge rock show but many other items are for sale too.

My husband was interested in purchasing some large chunks of turquoise which he found at tables owned by Native Americans who owned vast turquoise mines and had it for sale made into jewelry or cut and polished ready for use in the silver holdings. The town is called "Quartzite". It is at an intersection of two major highways and bulges with activity. Finding an empty space to park is a major achievement.

People from the Northern states who make a yearly ritual of going to the desert and exploring the flea markets and socializing in the sunshine are called "Snow Birds". It is not quite as comfortable as it sounds a lot of the time because of the crowded conditions. For instance, a couple of retired senior citizens had an altercation at a service station and a cane whacking sent one of them to the hospital. In another instance, the Post Office clerk shut the General Delivery window before a man could get his mail and he threw a rock through the window. I never heard how that turned out.

We heard of a State Park called "Crystal Mountain," where people can hike up the trail and find pieces of crystal. We decided to explore that place in our motor home. It was not too pleasant because I was having a problem with some food poisoning and was not able to leave the area. In the morning after we checked out we heard that a couple's pickup truck had been stolen. He had unhooked it from his trailer and left the motor running while he went back into the trailer preparing to take his wife to a doctor. Someone jumped into his running pick up and drove it away. I couldn't help thinking of the inconvenience it caused the couple.

In the meantime we met a man at our local flea market who told us of a couple of ranchette lots he had in Arizona that he was letting go because of unpaid taxes. We were interested in acquiring them which we did just as the time was running out. We paid the back taxes and gave the man some money for the lots and everyone was happy. We had no idea what the lots were like and he tried to describe them to us. We had bought "A pig in a poke", as the old saying goes. At least it would be a place to call our own and park under the wide open skies of Arizona.

Our next trip to Arizona the following winter we were able to find our lots. They were in the rough desert next to an eight foot deep arroyo where flash floods in the desert sent a river of huge boulders and rocks gushing like a torrent sweeping everything in its path. It was rocky and on a hillside but it was desert, complete with several varieties of cacti and desert plants. We went across a deep trench to drive there and got stuck when the battery bounced out of place and we had to walk back to town to get help. We went through a fence with a gate that held in the cattle that all gathered around us to look at the strange couple from the North West. It was over a mile to town.

The town consisted of a trailer court and rental cabins, a service station, a hardware store, a drug store and a night club and restaurant called the Ranch House.

One trip there and we learned about everyone in town, whether they were good or bad and we immediately felt like we were "in."

It was Christmas day and we had parked our small motor home at the trailer court and were standing in the yard trying to decide what we would do about Christmas dinner when a lady who lived there part time came and introduced herself and invited us to share Christmas dinner. It was a small trailer she and her husband had parked there for a convenient location and by the time dinner was served the walls were bulging with people they had invited to dinner. A couple from Yuma was bringing a ham and by the time they got there the dinner was very late in the day waiting for the ham to cook. It gave us plenty of time to get acquainted with the other couples and the day was pleasant.

That was the beginning of new friendships and experiences. We were invited to go on a convoy of four other motor homes to a huge flea market in Yuma Arizona at the dog race track. It was not our favorite place because we didn't think dogs should be exploited by racing them and betting on them. Then we regrouped and toured the place where the Yuma lady worked and were refreshed with cold beverages and plans for the next move.

Our wagon master was a tall skinny cowboy who never went anywhere without his guitar. He felt obligated to see to everyone's needs and never backed down from a fight. We circled our wagons on some Native American land across the Rio Grande River and were settled in for a few days, with a camp fire in the middle just like the pioneers.

I was resting in our motor home the second day when one of the ladies knocked on the door and said "You had better come out. The police want to see you," I thought she was joking and she assured me it was not a joke. When I opened the door I was looking down the barrel of a big police rifle. Not easily intimidated, I said to him, "Put that gun down. You are scaring me." He gave me a silly grin and did as he was told.

Unknown to the rest of us, the Border Patrol had been peering around the night before, checking the serial number on the generator and there had been a discussion with the wagon master that ended when another of our group spoke up from out of the darkness and the conversation ended. They had been watching us from afar the next day and finally made their move. We never knew what their reason was, as they did not search any of our motor homes looking for anything special. My husband thought it was a training session.

The experience to the desert was the beginning of wonderful friendships. Several of the couples came to Oregon to visit us in the mountains. When we tired of our ranchettes we were able to sell them quickly to someone else; another pig in a poke.

We didn't find everyone so friendly when we were on our way through the land. We stopped at a Laundromat and a young girl deliberately ran into me with the laundry cart. Without thinking I muttered something about reprisal but it was not heard by the adult in charge. It could have started a war. On another occasion a young woman in a store pushed a shopping cart into me and glared like I was the one at fault for being there. I tried to ignore it and consider the source. I believe that is what is referred to as "turning the other cheek." I try to think that I handled it properly.

Snow birding was our ritual for several years until we discovered the comfort of being home in our warm house. Old snow birds reluctantly stay closer to the roost.

TRIAL BY JURY

Some people seem to feel honored by being requested to do Jury duty. Someone has to do it. You cannot refuse to be available for Jury duty without a statement from your doctor, or have a very good and legitimate reason to refuse.

The only time I was notified that I was to serve on a jury I had a legitimate reason to refuse. I did not feel like I was jury material. It was a time in my life when I was expected to be irrational and unreasonable according to tradition. It never got to the point that I needed my doctor's statement but I had no doubt that he would agree with my assessment of the situation.

I answered the summons in a hand written letter explaining that I would not be a good juror because of my emotional and compassionate nature. I would take the problems home with me and always wonder if I should have felt differently about certain points. I was certain my doctor would agree with me. I insinuated that I was a crack pot and had no business deciding some one's fate.

My husband and I were involved in trial by jury to recover material that we felt was wrongly taken from us. Everything looked good for us until the opposition resorted to witnesses that told untruths. We knew they were lying and they knew they were lying but those on the jury didn't have any way of knowing.

There were other things that seemed amiss in the jury selection, such as one of them being a close neighbor of the defendant. I didn't think it was a proper selection but our own attorney didn't seem to think it was significant. Perhaps it was a normal feeling but we felt like we had been shafted. We were on the wrong side of the tracks from the beginning. We were ordinary working people trying to hold our own with a big name around town.

When I hear of some of the outcome of jury trials it makes me wonder what became of the adage, innocent until proven guilty. The jurors are compelled to make a decision based on reasonable doubt. Even after the trials are over some of the jurors are left wondering if they made a good decision. There was doubt in their mind but they still were pressured to make a decision and they did, whether it was right or wrong. I am sure a lot of people are plagued for life by their findings.

I read recently about a woman sentenced to twenty years in prison for firing a warning shot during a domestic problem. It sounds unbelievable. Justice? There must be something I don't understand.

ORPHAN HUMMING BIRD

A man I know, a good friend, works as a mechanic for a construction company. His hard workings hands are capable of doing many things besides repairing greasy engines for large pieces of equipment. Through the goodness of his generous heart he offers his services to help others who are in need of food or other necessities. There seems to be no limit to his generosity.

The kindness of this person does not stop with people in need. It extends to helpless creatures no matter where and what they are, like the humming bird's nest the wind blew out of a tree. It contained two naked baby birds, one of them still alive with its beak open and peeping for a drop of nectar from its forlorn mother. He carefully gathered the nest with the surviving baby and took it home with him.

How does a person take care of a baby humming bird? It requires warmth and nectar and kindness and someone to be the bird sitter in his absence. No problem there, his family was caught up in the care of the little bird. Nectar was provided by some sugar in water and dropped into the open beak from a tooth pick.

The little bird survived and grew some feathers. At that point its caretaker decided he had done what was required of him. He contacted an animal and bird sanctuary and the people there agreed to take the baby bird and see to its maturity so that it could be turned loose in the wild. They later called him and told him the good care was successful and the humming bird had been turned loose to enjoy its life as the beautiful free creature it was meant to be.

Recently I heard that this kind person was caring for a wounded Banty hen that had a close call with a raccoon one night. She was roosting in a tree in his yard and ended up torn and blind in one eye. Now he keeps her in a cage until she gets well enough to be put with other chickens.

I am sure there will be many gold stars for this kind man.

WEATHER PREDICTIONS

Some old timers I knew took pride in their ability to predict the weather for the coming winters. One of them looked at the acorn crop. Another one kept track of the bird migration. I often heard it said "It is going to be an early fall", or "It' going to be an early spring." or vice versa.

I am not very good at prediction weather but I can see the results before, during and after it happens. In recent years I can feel it in my bones. I find that I am not alone there. In fact, I read an article written by an M.D. that stated he had made an investigation about painful bones and the weather and found it to be true. The tissues around the joints swell, causing pressure on the nerves. That gives us some ammunition when people insinuate that it is all in our heads.

My hearing impairment leaves me with peaceful, quiet nights. The house could collapse around my head and I would probably still think it was in fine order. It has its advantages when I don't want to hear something. By looking out the bedroom window I can see if it is raining by the light shining on the tin roof over the storage shed. It is completely dull except when it is raining.

It is easy to know if the wind has been blowing hard by the dead oak limbs lying around the yard. Very soon the deer come and strip the limbs of the moss, so I have to make my conclusions early in the day. After the deer eat the moss the limbs disappear into the mulch of dead grass and leaves.

There have been a few occasions when there was no doubt about the temperature. My husband and our son and I made the trip to Alaska on the Alcan Highway to visit our daughter and son-in-law. We had a large van and slept in sleeping bags. Our son had to fly home because of work duties and my husband and I made the trip back to Oregon a few days later. Our body heat was so important and necessary that we didn't think of letting it escape by changing into sleeping clothes. For about five nights we just crawled into our sleeping bags, perfectly content and unashamed that we were starting to smell.

That was the month of January and it was not surprising that the weather was cold. We could see the creeks and rivers freezing over more each day. We drove for miles hoping to have a nice breakfast. There was no restaurant and all we could come up with was a box of Hi Ho crackers at a wide spot along the road. No problem, there would be another place down the road. Way, way down the road! We really wanted some service and a refill on the coffee but the American tourists were not nearly as important to the restaurant staff as the work crew that was having breakfast. We left, trying to count our blessings which were badly frozen about that time.

Another frigid trip I recall was when my son and I drove to Boise Idaho in the middle of January. It was a getaway trip shortly after my husband passed away. My son Belongs to a Jeep Club and knows every camp site and hot springs through the desert of Eastern Oregon. We finally arrived at a special hot springs late at night and he built a fire and cooked some burger steaks for a quick meal. Fortunately he was well prepared for camping with his cold weather Arctic sleeping bags. He goes to the high mountains during elk hunting season and is a survivalist for that kind of life. He made me comfortable in my sleeping bag under the canopy over his truck bed and I had to be very careful to not let a bit of air in to spoil the comfort. If I was a praying woman I would have asked to be spared having to get out of my sleeping bag that cold, frigid night. Fortunately I made it through the night.

In the morning when we expected to make some campfire coffee we discovered that the gallon jug of water we had in the ice chest was frozen solid. It was onward to the next wide spot along the road several hours later when we finally had hot coffee and a bowl of very good soup.

On the return trip we were able to have a picnic of canned beef stew a few hours from home. It tasted very good when we finally found a place free of snow where we could get off the highway.

Our meteorologists do a fine job keeping us informed about the weather. We are always quick to point out the errors. That is human nature, to make mistakes and find fault. We can always stick a wet finger in the air to see which way the wind is blowing. We can always look out the window to see if the rain is dripping off the roof. Who needs their predictions! We will find out soon enough when the roads are flooded and we lose our electricity.

Here's to the weather person and the crew that comes along to pick up the pieces.

FINAL OBSERVATIONS

Life is an interesting adventure when it is connected with the spiritual aspect of the world in addition to the earthly components. Discovering all the unknown truths that surround us makes a new episode of every day. I have enjoyed the discoveries as they occurred and the insights into the world that have been gained by the connection with the Spirit Guides. Each new way to communicate only adds a greater dimension to my knowledge and understanding.

From the first little steps with the pendulum and chart, the addition of the drum as a communication tool, and the communication with the Spirit Guides, my knowledge gained status and I have been able to help others through those tools.

We all have the ability to expand our horizons and make our corner of the world a better place.

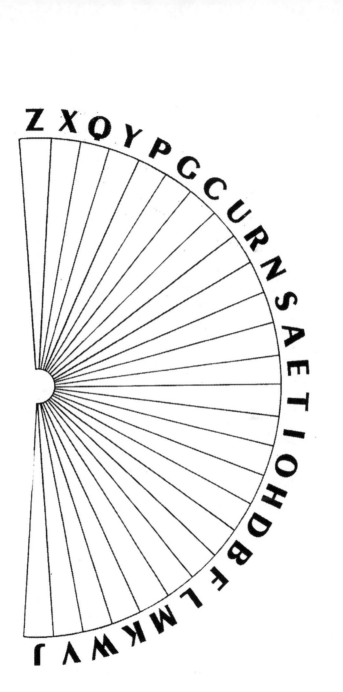